THE HISTORY OF MAN *(sort of)*
From Adam to Atom

By

Saul P. Davis, M.D.

ISBN: 1-4140-0415-X (e-book)
ISBN: 1-4140-0416-8 (Paperback)

This book is printed on acid free paper.

1stBooks - rev. 10/29/03

TABLE OF CONTENTS

PREFACE

The biographies detailed in this book represent months of research in libraries and personal interviews.

The History Department of Boston College has been very cooperative in reviewing and editing the material. Every statement has been authenticated and warranted for accuracy by the Vilnius University School of Education.

You will find the book very informative and interesting, or you won't.

CHAPTER ONE

<u>ADAM</u>

After God finished creating the universe in six days, he took the next day off to relax and contemplate his handiwork. He was very pleased with the result, but after a few days, he began to become restless and started to look for other things to be done. He noted a number of small depressions in the land, and wondered what to do about them. He had already created the vast oceans of water, which gave him the idea of filling the depressions with water, thus forming thousands of large and small ponds surrounded by the trees he had previously created. This took many hours of hard work, but was completed by the end of the second six-day period of work. After a prolonged rest period, he again began feeling restless and he wished he had someone to talk to and share his handiwork.

After a long period of solitude, he thought of creating a "man" with two legs so that he could walk and appreciate his surroundings. He would have to have some intelligence- (but not too much) so that he could take care of himself and communicate with his Maker.

The more God thought about this, the more he was convinced it would be good to have some company, and they could pass the time playing games and planning future adventures.

After working out the details of making "man" self-sufficient, he realized he must supply him with food to maintain his strength. So it was an easy matter to start vegetables and fruit growing and he stacked the ponds with swimming creatures and the woods with walking and crawling eatables.　Of course they would have to be instilled with life so they would stay fresh.

The stage was now set for the major enterprise of creating "man".　Since this was the first man He ever made, He started with a few samples but He soon discovered they had faults, -like two left feet, a head too small for a brain, hands with no fingers, a brain which could control motion, but couldn't think.　After making the necessary corrections, God felt ready to create the first man (but He always worried about man's intelligence).

He went ahead with the production that took six more days.　When He was finished, he looked with admiration at his creation and finally he breathed life into the first human being and called him "Adam."

Adam opened his eyes, stood up and looked around. He was amazed at the beauty he beheld and asked aloud "Where am I?"　God answered, "You are on earth and all this is yours, as long as you take care of it and follow my instructions." "Who are You?" asked Adam. "I am the creator of all this land and you." "You can stay here, rent free, as long as you don't mess up the neighborhood."

You can do anything you want to amuse yourself. You can hunt, fish, swim in the lake, play with the animals, but stay away from a small four-legged animal, black with a white stripe on the back; it could cause an undesirable effect.

Adam set out to explore his new home. The beauty of the land, the trees and foliage overwhelmed him. He became friendly with the animals, and was always careful not to do any damage. God was pleased with Adam's behavior and always warned him if there was any approaching danger.

Adam was happy with his life but after a while his existence was becoming routine and he started to look for some excitement. He felt something was missing from his life but didn't know what it was. He discussed this with

4

God who was sorry to hear Adam's complaint. Adam tried to make the best of the situation, but the feeling of loneliness became worse.

One day, while discussing the cause of his depression, God told him he would like to get him some Prozac but his insurance would not cover it.

Adam thought out loud that if there was another person around to talk to and play games with, it might help. God was surprised at this, but the thought of another person had not occurred to him, but it might be the answer and he would give it some thought. A few days later, God appeared before Adam and said "Adam I have thought about your idea, and I agree." "Another person would be wonderful for you, and it would give me another plan for the future." "I will start work for a companion for you right away."

True to His word, in the middle of the night a little later, Adam was awakened from his sleep to hear God's voice saying, "Adam, here is your new friend." Adam opened his eyes, and a light shone on another person. Adam was happy beyond words at the sight of a beautiful person who was standing there smiling at him. He jumped up and inspected the new companion, and he said to God, "This is wonderful." "He is like me, but not quite the same." God replied, "This is not another man, this is a woman." "The difference is obvious, and I will explain the reasons later."

"But in the meantime, I forbid either of your to touch the other." "You can talk and play games, but if either of you touches the other, you will be severely punished. Your new friend's name is Eve," and God was gone.

Of course neither one had ever spoken to another person before, and they were both reluctant to talk at first, but soon started to become acquainted, and Adam asked Eve "Do you come here often?" "No, replied Eve, but I will now that you're here." They walked down to the pond for a drink, and sat and talked all the time being careful not to touch each other. Adam noted that when he was close to Eve, a change took place in his body which had never happened before.

He couldn't understand this, but it embarrassed him, so he picked a leaf off a nearby fig tree and tied it around his waist. Eve tried not to notice this, but to make him feel more comfortable, she tied a fig leaf around her own waist.

As the days went by, the couple became more familiar with each other and enjoyed talking and swimming in the nearby pond. Adam hunted and brought back food that Eve prepared. After eating, they let out the iguana that they had adopted and went to sleep on the straw mats they had made. Very often at this time, Adam noted that same change in his body that had occurred the first time he met Eve, and later it occurred almost anytime he was close to her. She, in turn felt a strange type of aching in her lower abdomen when Adam was close. However, aware of God's warning, they never touched each other.

God respected their privacy, and rarely became involved in their activities. One day, God spoke to them and said "You have behaved very well and respected my creations, and as a reward, I have arranged for you to have a vacation at a very nice resort at the edge of the Greatwater, called the Garden of Eden." "Go and enjoy it, stay as long as you like, but remember, NO TOUCHING!"

Adam and Eve were glad to go to a new place after having stayed in the same place for a long time. In preparation for the trip, Adam picked a new leaf from the fig tree that he tied on and took another one as a spare. Eve also wanted something new to wear, but as a change picked a leaf from the grapevine, and replaced the old covering. Adam said she looked nice in the grape leaf, so she plucked a few more for future use. They started out heading toward the setting sun knowing there would be food and water along the way. They stopped every night and slept on beds of soft grass side by side. At these times he noted the same alteration in his body, and he felt a longing to reach out and touch Eve. But he heeded God's warning and restrained himself. One night while preparing their bedding, a snake slithered out of the brush, and to their amazement, he spoke to them. He asked where they were going, and they replied that God had sent them to the Garden of Eden, and they told him of God's commandment about touching. The snake laughed, and said, "Don't pay any attention to that, God is against anything that is fun. He has a list of Ten Commandments that he scares all the residents with, but he's basically good, and would never do anything to hurt you. Go ahead to your garden, and touch all you want, and have a good time."

He then slithered back into the bush. The couple looked at each other in disbelief, and didn't know what to make of the revelation. Adam said he respected God's warning and was afraid to cross Him. Eve was also hesitant at first, but when she saw Adam's fig leaf stand straight out, she knew the question was settled. That night, after preparing their bedding, they lay down side by side. She started out by touching Adam on the shoulder, gently and hesitatingly stroked his arm. Adam felt an overwhelming desire to see what Eve felt like, and he was surprised and pleased by the smooth warmth of her skin and they both continued their mutual exploration, until they finally ended in an unexpected state of euphoric exhaustion.

After a period of pleasant recovery, Adam wondered aloud why, if God gave them the gift of such a wonderful experience, why did he forbid them to use it. Eve did not have the answer-and although there have been many ridiculous postulations, no reasonable answer has yet been forthcoming. Instead, in defiance of their Master's warning, they became the parents of two sons Caine and Able (who provide another chapter in the history of man). It is obvious now that without Adam and Eve's transgression, none of us would be here today. Adam and Eve were banished from The Garden of Eden Resort, but after wandering around, they finally settled in a pleasant clearing at the edge of the Mediterranean Sea and raised a family.

CHAPTER TWO
ABRAHAM

Abraham, the father of the Hebrew religion, was born and spent his early years in a town called UR, near the Euphrates River. As he grew up, he began moving around and spent most of his adult life around the town of Hebron. At a very early age, he began hearing messages from God. While the other boys his age were out playing "kick the pomegranate," and chasing maidens, Abraham was home communicating with God through angels. The other people in the area worshipped artificial Gods or statues or had no conception of what God was. As he grew older, his love and respect for what he believed was the only true God, who created the world and man, became the center of his life.

One day while relaxing and meditating along the Jordan River, he met and fell in love with a beautiful young lady named Sarah. After a short courtship, during which he showered her with sheep, pigs, olives, and dandelions, they were married with God's blessing. They lived happily for a while, but Abraham desperately wanted a son, but Sarah was unable to produce one. Abraham became very depressed, because he wanted a son to continue to preach the wonders of God. Poor Sarah felt responsible for Abraham's anguish, and she suggested that she would step aside and Abraham could Marry Hagar, their maid.

At first he was appalled, but he decided to see how God felt about it. To his surprise, God thought it was a pretty good idea as long as Sarah didn't mind. And He would do His Best to make Hagar fertile. With everyone's consent, Abraham went off with Hager and after an appropriate time, she became pregnant and eventually gave birth to a son, Ishmael.

With this accomplished, Abraham bought Hagar a nicely furnished cave with a built-in microwave, a freezer stocked with instant dinners and pizzas, and a pre-owned camel for transportation. He also gave her custody of Ishmael.

All the time, Abraham was in touch with God showing his respect and worshipping him with praise and thanks and offered to do anything God wanted of him. God replied that Abraham was a devoted believer and would be made the leader of a great nation, and his descendants would cover the earth and would be blessed with God's protection. He only wanted Abraham to be a good man and respect and love all his fellow man. He made a covenant with Abraham to follow His teachings and to distinguish Abraham from non-believers, he would instruct him in the rite of circumcision. When God told Abraham how it was to be done, Abraham exclaimed, "You want me to cut my

WHAT?" "You must be kidding." God quieted him down and said, "If you do as I told you, and have all your male descendants do the same, I will treat you as my Chosen People." You will have all the land you need for all your followers who will multiply like the sands of the sea and have MY blessings." All this time Sarah prayed to Abraham's God that she should become pregnant and start the line of descendants which had been predicted.

After Abraham's operation was healed, in answer to Sarah's prayers, she finally gave birth to a son they named Isaac. Abraham gave thanks to his God and offered up a lamb as a sacrifice. Isaac thrived and eventually married and had a son, Jacob, and the grandparents were overjoyed and thankful. Three years later the tranquility of the family was overwhelmed when an Angel from God appeared before Abraham and told him that God commanded him to sacrifice his older son to prove his fidelity to God. Abraham was overwhelmed with grief at the thought of killing his beloved Isaac who had grown to be a fine, obedient son. Abraham did not mention the angel's visit to Sarah or his sons, but after wrestling with his conscience, he could not go against the commandment of his sacred and beloved God. So one day he took his sacrificial equipment and took Isaac by the hand and ascended the mountain to the usual site of animal sacrifice. He tied the bewildered boy to the alter, raised the sharpened knife, and was about to drive it into his son, when he suddenly heard a loud voice call out, "Stop!" "Do not harm the boy, untie him." Abraham turned, and to his amazement, there stood a female angel with anger in her eyes. "Why were you going to kill the lad?" "God told me to do it," said Abraham. "Oh sure, and I'm the tooth fairy," replied the angel. Then, softening her demeanor, she admitted that God had sent her to comfort Abraham, and tell him that he had proved his loyalty to God, and he would be blessed for the rest of his life, along with all his followers who shared his love and devotion to God.

This act confirmed God's covenant in return for Abraham's cooperation. He would promise his followers their freedom and all the land they would need to expand and prosper.

Isaac, Abraham's son by Sarah, carried on his father's teachings and his examples of respect and love for his God. Isaac subsequently married Rebecca, and they had a pair of twin sons, Jacob and Esau. Jacob carried on Abraham's traditional relationship with God and strengthened the integrity of the Hebrew community and their settlement in Palestine.

CHAPTER THREE
MOSES

During the period of the Hebrew's slavery in Egypt, the Pharaoh who was very cruel told his subjects, that the Jewish slaves were getting out of hand and had to be punished. He said he was planning to kill the first-born Jewish child in each family. One Jewish mother had just given birth to a son, and was afraid he would be killed. So she placed him in a basket with some clean diapers, a bottle of Pepsi and a package raisins and floated him down the Nile River. The next day, the Pharaoh's daughter heard him crying and saw him in the bulrushes along the shore and

picked him up. He asked who she was, and she told him.
"I'm the Pharaoh's daughter," and she was going to take
him home. She named him "Moses," which was Arabic for
Moses. As time went by, he grew to be a clever young
man. He became a favorite of the Pharaoh's family and was
granted special favors. He learned about his background,
and he became upset and antagonistic as he grew old
enough to realize that slavery was not the way his people
should be treated. He tried to turn the Egyptian people
against the Pharaoh by spreading a rumor that he was gay,
and the princess had AIDS. But this did not impress the
people, because most of them practiced sexual aberrations
themselves.

Moses soon found out that he could not expect any
help from the population, and he would have to deal with
Pharaoh himself. Moses had been satisfied with his
situation since he was making big money as a dealer in the
Cairo Casino. This made him very popular with the local
maidens, but he was becoming more concerned and
depressed by the plight of his people. He tried to convince

Pharaoh he would be better off if he let the Hebrews go, because the captives might be planning a revolution. He said he heard that they had hidden weapons of destruction and were getting ready to use them to obtain their freedom. Pharaoh was not impressed saying he had inspectors looking for such weapons who had found nothing but a few piles of rocks and some foul smelling animals which could not produce enough toxic gas to cause anymore than a little nausea.

One evening while playing Gin Rummy with the Pharaoh, Moses said that the Hebrews had a secret weapon named God who was ready to help them to escape. Pharaoh countered by saying he did not fear anything he couldn't see, and he had an ally who was ready to supply him with destructive weapons. Under prodding by Moses, Pharaoh named the co-terrorist Sadaam Insane the violent head of a nearby country named Deception. They appeared to be at an impasse, and the Egyptian leader would not agree to a mediator. Moses knew he had to move quickly, so he called upon God and explained the situation and the need for the Jews to be freed quickly because they were becoming anxious and he was afraid they would do something that would make things worse for themselves. God promised he would act soon in view of his covenant with Abraham and the Hebrews. In a few days Moses found a message on his E Mail outlining a plan consisting of ten plagues that would break down the will of the Egyptians. True to his word, the next day there was a tremendous invasion of flies, mosquitoes and vermin taking over the whole country. They were inside houses and outside. They were in people's mouths, noses, ears and all other apertures. It rapidly became more than a nuisance, and the citizens begged the Pharaoh to do something. He put in a hasty call to Sadaam Insane for help, who responded by sending 3000 gallons of RAID by UPS, and the natives set about spraying their houses, lawns and farms. When the RAID ran out, they re-ordered more until all the pests were gone and the cleanup commenced. Pharaoh was upset, but showed no sign of capitulating. In fact, he was pleased because the value of the stock he owned in RAID, doubled in one week.

God noted all this and decided on another plague-an invasion of frogs. Again, they were everywhere, in houses, farms and roads. When people walked, there a constant squishing of frogs being crushed, chariots and buses would leave trails of crushed frogs. However, the Egyptian women were mostly good cooks, and soon they began scraping up barrels of frogs and preparing frog's legs, cooked, barbecued, stewed, roasted and frogburgers. The men loved the new delicacy, and were disappointed when all the frogs were gone.

God figured he would try something more dramatic. Accordingly, a few days later an epidemic of boils appeared on the skin of almost all the Egyptian people. They appeared on the faces, bodies and extremities of people of all ages. They were painful, full of puss and unsightly. Pharaoh panicked and the local doctors had no way of treating disease. The Pharaoh contacted his sinister ally Saddam Insane, and almost by return UPS 3000 vials of penicillin were delivered. The local medics, witch doctors, and HMO representatives began injecting everyone with the drug. Almost immediately, the epidemic began to subside, and within a few days the plague ended. God tried other plagues, and they were all countered by various measures until God and Moses scheduled a conference to make a definitive plan to break the will of Pharaoh and his followers. After much thought and consideration and soul searching, God decided he would send the Angel of death to kill the first-born son of each Egyptian family. At first Moses was appalled by the thought of killing innocent children, but God said that Moses' people had been enslaved too long and Pharaoh had been intransigent, and extreme measures were needed. He picked the first night of Passover to perform the executions and He told Moses to tell all the Hebrew households to kill a lamb and paint the doorposts with the lamb's blood, so the angel of death would know to pass over the Jewish homes and not kill the wrong people.

When the Egyptian families awoke the next morning, and saw what had happened, they were distraught with grief as was Pharaoh, who finally decided if the Hebrews could call upon a force such as this, it was time to call a truce and release the Jews from slavery. Moses called a meeting of the representatives of all the Jewish tribes to plan for the departure. Of course all the freed people were ecstatic and started packing for their return to the Promised Land. Moses urged the people to hurry before Pharaoh changed his mind, but many of the women had to do last minute shopping and others had hair or nail appointments.

Some of the women wanted to bake bread to eat on the way, but Moses convinced them not to wait for the bread not to fully bake, so they took it "unleavened" and it was known as Matzo. They hurried out through the open gates in a long stream of borrowed camels, donkeys, hurriedly made cars, scooters and old SUV's, but most walked.

After two days of travel, they approached a body of water that appeared on Moses' AAA map as the Red Sea, which was blocking their way. As Moses looked around for an escape route, he saw a cloud of dust rising behind him, and he knew at once that Pharaoh had indeed changed his mind, and his soldiers were coming after them. He knew they were trapped, and had to find some escape path quickly. He also knew the only person in the world who had experience in this type of situation, so he immediately sent an urgent fax to Cecile B. Demille in California. Almost immediately Moses received, by return fax, an explanation of the rescue procedure. Moses immediately instituted the remedy, and everyone was amazed to see the water begin to separate and leave a dry path. Moses and his followers hurried through the path, but when the Egyptian Army tried to follow, the waters closed in and drowned them. Moses gathered all the people around him, and they offered thanks to their God for allowing them to escape safely.

Now they found themselves in a desert as far as they could see. There were no signposts or landmarks, but Moses felt that they should go north. However, he confided to his close friend Moishe Ben Pipick that in his haste to leave Egypt he had forgotten his compass and didn't know North from South. They had to make a choice, so they decided to toss a shekel. It came up heads, so they told all the waiting escapees to follow them hoping they had made the correct choice. After traveling forty years through the desert with only an occasional donkey burger or braised camel ribs, they came to a mountain they named "Sinai". It contained soil, rocks, trees and a few streams. All the time they were trudging through the hot desert, the travelers were becoming more and more unhappy and began faulting Moses and even God who had led them astray. One of them, who had attended astronomy school, insisted that they had been traveling south. Moses grudgingly admitted that he had probably been a little off the mark, and after a little rest they would start again in the right direction. They stopped at the bottom of Mt. Sinai and there was much dissention and anger directed at Moses and God. Suddenly a black cloud formed over the mountain followed by loud thunder and vivid lightning, and God's loud voice announced that he wanted to see Moses at the top of the mountain.

Always obedient, Moses donned his poncho and climbing boots and told his people to behave and rest and he would return with God's words. Moses was gone for a month, during which the people were becoming more and more rebellious and some even renounced God and made a statue of a large animal and pretended to pray to it. They made wine out of grapes they had grown and soon began to become too friendly toward each other. Finally there was more booming thunder and Moses appeared carrying a stone tablet containing Hebrew writing. When he saw and heard how the people were carrying on, he became furious and smashed the tablet to the ground and berated the offenders and told them that God had sent them a list of forbidden activities that they had already defied. He was pacified by some of the more dedicated followers, and he agreed to go up to the copier and get another list of the commandments, but if this unacceptable behavior continued, God would deal with them severely and give them a prolonged time out. He again ascended the mountain and returned in two days with a new stone tablet on which was etched God's ten commandments. He read them to the congregation and explained the meaning of a few words that might not be familiar to some of the less knowledgeable characters. He announced that they were start out for the Promised Land and this time there would be no problems because he had received an AAA map.

It took them twenty years to reach the outskirts of the land of Canaan, but unfortunately the whole effort to escape from bondage followed by the long journey and mental stress was too much for the 120-year-old Moses and he died without ever setting foot on the Promised Land. He was buried after a modest ceremony and God appointed Moshie Ben Pipick to carry the Ten Commandments and lead the people into the land of Israel.

In a fairly short time, the people became adjusted to their new surroundings and freedom. They mixed with the local inhabitants most of whom had no religion or scruples. They rejected the Ten Commandments and tried to introduce the newcomers into their way of life. Many of them settled in two cities fairly close together named Sodom and Gomorrah. The behavior and morals of most of the natives disregarded order and restraint and promoted crime and sexual misbehavior. God was furious with their activities and threatened to severely punish the participants. The native people did not believe in God or any restraint on their activities and continued with their egregious behavior. Finally God sent word that the two cities were to be destroyed. The prophet pleaded with God that he would be killing innocent people, but there was no other way of eliminating the sexual perversion that was named for the city of Sodom. The only way was to destroy the two cities, which was thoroughly accomplished. A few residents managed to survive and over a period of time moved to different cities and were absorbed into their new surroundings. Their abnormal behavior was gradually revived and persists to this day. Gamorrahmy apparently never became very popular and there is no evidence that it has ever been revived. Apparently once the women took it into their heads to resume the abnormal sexual behavior it was difficult to change their minds. The men also found it hard for them to give up their old habits, but they were able to find a handy substitute so the practice was reestablished and spread around the world. Gammorrahmy was never revived except for some occasional late night TV. In spite of all this Moses stands out as one of the worlds great leaders.

CHAPTER FOUR
<u>JESUS</u>

In Southern Judea a young Jewish carpenter named Joseph inherited a small business which manufactured custom made chairs from his father. The business was fairly successful, and Joseph met and fell in love with a pretty seventeen year old girl named Mary. After a brief courtship, they became engaged, but never married because Joseph had ED and knew he probably could not have children. They got along well, until one day Mary told Joseph that she was pregnant. "What??," he exclaimed. "Have you been hanging out with those used camel salesmen, down on Camel Row?" "Oh Joseph," she sobbed. "How could you think I could be unfaithful to you?" "Well who is the father?" "God, did it," said Mary. "Oh sure, I heard that one before." Mary pleaded convincingly, and Joseph grudgingly accepted her story. Mary said later, "I thought you would be pleased to know that our child will have the first true Godfather. "That placated Joseph, and they resumed their normal relationship. After a short period of morning sickness, Mary felt very well and developed a good appetite for ice cream and pickles. After five months, she had gained fifteen pounds and was becoming self-conscious about her appearance. So one day Joseph bought her a maternity toga that made her very happy.

At about that time the Roman emperor issued an edict that all citizens must come to Jerusalem to register for a census that was being carried out to determine the number and party affiliation of all residents.

Joseph and Mary knew they had to hurry since her obstetrician had told her she was due in a month. They packed their essential traveling necessities including her daily vitamins on their donkey, and started the trip to Jerusalem.

As they approached a small town just South of their destination, they passed a sign saying "Welcome to Bethlehem." By this time Mary was starting to have labor pains, so Joseph went on ahead to find an inn where they could stay, but the only one in town was a Holiday Inn, but the desk clerk said all the rooms were booked, because today is the holiday of Christmas, and he said there were no vacancies anywhere in town. He suggested a small cave just off the Main St. where they probably could stay. In answer to Joseph's question, he said that the only obstetrician in Bethlehem was off to Beersheba where he was performing a cesarean section and would not return for several days. Joseph returned to where he had left Mary and found her very uncomfortable with frequent labor pains. They settled in the small cavern that the locals called

"Manger Inn." Joseph rounded up some straw and spread it out for Mary to lie on. He bought some clean cloths at a dry good store in town and made a fire to boil the essential water. Mary's labor pains became very frequent and she cried out with each one. Joseph could tell that the birth was coming quickly, and he didn't know anything about delivery, so he went out to the main street and brought back a policeman and a taxi driver, knowing they had experience in emergency deliveries of babies. They tended to their work efficiently, and presently a baby's cry was heard and Joseph proudly held up his son who appeared to be well formed and healthy. Mary was now comfortable and made tea with the boiled water. Some observers declared they saw a halo over the head of the baby whom they named "Jesus." Three smart men appeared out of nowhere and announced that the baby was blessed and would become the leader of men.

The baby flourished and Joseph and Mary wanted to get out of the cold weather of the Bethlehem winter. They thought of going to Florida, but instead went to Egypt where it was warm and they could get on their donkey that was the least expensive transportation available. They stayed at the Cairo Hilton for forty days before starting the long trip home to Nazareth. By this time baby Jesus was thriving on Mary's nursing and at age six months was beginning to talk. The little family set out. After loading up the donkey with their sparse possessions and a map from the ACA (Asian Camel Assoc.), they crossed the desert northward until they reached Beersheba in Southern Palestine. After purchasing supplies, they continued northward through Jerusalem and Samaria to Nazareth.

During Jesus' adolescence, he was a bright and studious Jewish scholar who learned about his background dating back to David. When he approached his mid twenties, he began having ideas about human behavior and began speaking before religious and civil gatherings. His ideas were not always in keeping with other citizens', and he frequently appeared with bruises on his face from turning the other cheek. He never had any prolonged feuds, because he loved his enemies. His reputation as a public speaker spread and his audiences were impressed with his calm and self-assured attitude even though some of his ideas were not always readily accepted. Most of his public lectures were held in the vicinity of the Sea of Galilee, and he became familiar with many of the fisherman. One day, he met a fisherman who had empty nets and appeared discouraged. Jesus asked his name, and he said "Peter." Jesus told Peter to forget about fishing and come with him, and he would find peace and contentment, but first he must change his clothes because his fishy smell might repel the followers. Peter did as he was told, and the two of them started out on a tour of the neighboring towns. Peter was amazed at the fantastic tricks and unbelievable feats his mentor was able to perform. At one stop a large wedding was taking place, but the bride's father did not have much money to spend. All he could afford was a loaf of bread and two fish. Jesus saw the desperation on the father's face and without hesitation he changed the two loaves into five thousand and tapped a nearby stone which had had a trickle of water coming out of it, and changed the water into enough wine to satisfy the whole assembly. The people were amazed, and the father was so grateful for saving his daughter's marriage that he fell to his knees and kissed Jesus' feet. Jesus picked up the man and told him he had many other tricks he could perform, and to watch the local papers and he could attend other performances. But before leaving he told the wedding guests they could insure happy futures if they attended his services, were good to each other, and followed the words of God. Then Peter and Jesus left to loud cheering and exclamations of gratitude.

Two days later as they were walking along the shore of Galilee, they saw a man standing knee deep in the water who appeared to be drowning another man. Jesus hurried over to see what was happening, and he cried out to the aggressor, "Stop! Why are you drowning this man?" He responded, "My name is John, and I am baptizing this man to cleanse him of his sins so that he will be acceptable for entry into heaven on the day of judgment." Jesus said, "That is very commendable." "Would you have time to baptize me and my companion?" John said, "I know who you are, I've heard of your wonderful tricks, and I would be honored to baptize you." Accordingly he dunked the two subjects into the cold water and said a prayer. He noticed that Peter was shivering and John said "I know it is cold here, but I am planning to build an indoor pool, which will be larger and warm, so that people can swim and frolic in the water while waiting to be baptized." Jesus dried off, touched John's head, and said a prayer for his health and for his new undertaking.

The two travelers proceeded north to Nazareth and as they approached the small town, they came upon a small funeral procession, which was proceeding slowly toward the town cemetery. At the head of the procession, walked a young sad looking woman who was crying and praying quietly to herself. The scene touched Jesus and he approached the young woman and offered his condolences. The mourner said that this was her cousin Lazarus who died four days ago, and although his religion requires burial within twenty-four hours, she was not emotionally prepared to do it. Jesus told her he would try to help, so he walked over to the body that was wrapped in a prayer shawl. He touched Lazarus on the forehead and said a brief prayer. To everyone's amazement, Lazarus opened his eyes, looked around and said, "What's going on?" He was told he had died four days ago and was revived by this stranger. "Four days ago?" "Why wasn't I buried before this?' "This must be God's will, said the young cousin." Lazarus stood up a little weak and walked over to Jesus embraced him, and kissed his hand. He asked what he could do to show his gratitude, and Jesus said all he wanted was for him and the members of his family to be good to one another, pray to God, and love your enemies. The people looked at each other in surprise, but no one questioned the edict out of respect for the gifted stranger.

After going on a little way, Peter said he was growing tired and wanted to return to see how his former fishing associates were getting along. They parted ways, but Peter said he would spread the words of Jesus' teachings and his magic performances and his devotion to God and he would urge the people to love and respect him because he had to be a messenger from God.

Peter had heard about Jesus' birth by a virgin mother and in view of the miracles he had seen performed, and listening to his sermons, he was convinced that Jesus was indeed the Son of God. Peter traveled throughout the area, promoting the future arrival of Jesus to spread and demonstrate his magic. He was an excellent PR man and was successful in converting many of the residents to believe in the divinity of Jesus and he created the name of "Christianity." Many of the people who saw him and heard his sermons, if not convinced of his relationship to God, recognized him as the greatest magician of all time. In view of such unexplained events such as reviving dead people, restoring sight in blind people, converting loaves of bread into thousands, converting water to wine, curing leprosy and many other magic feats. Jesus was a polished orator and advocated rules of conduct that would promote peace and cooperation among the citizens of the community. However, some did not agree with the concept of loving people who sought to do them harm, and not responding when attacked. He did promote himself as the Son of God, just as many others before him had, but had proved to be false. However, Jesus was so convincing and in view of the previous prophecies of the coming of God's son, that he was able to establish a large growing and devoted following. Inevitably the Emperor of the Roman Empire who had invaded and occupied the whole Palestine area recognized his fame and notoriety in Rome. This raised the question of the danger of this newcomer posing a threat to the stability of the occupying Roman administration. Accordingly, the Emperor sent Pontius Pilate to Jerusalem to put an end to the possible rebellion. After a pseudo trial, Pontius Pilate sentenced Jesus to death by crucifixion. This was accomplished by extreme cruelty. After Jesus had died, his body was removed from the cross and placed in a cave at the base of the mount. A large rock was placed across the opening of the cave for safekeeping.

The next day, people came to remove the body, but found that the rock had been moved, and the body was gone. Was this another magic trick of the master magician? This has never been answered, but a few weeks later two ladies shopping at Wallmarts in downtown Jerusalem, reported seeing Jesus buying some pomegranates. Other people claimed they had sighted him, but these were never confirmed.

Peter was overwrought but continued his advocacy of the holiness of Jesus and his relationship to God. His efforts were so fruitful that he and Paul formed a viable, growing religion in spite of Rome's constant threat to Peter who was to become the first Pope.

John the Baptist had been arrested and put in prison for his association with Jesus. At a large social function, held by Pilate and other Roman officials, there was a beautiful young dancer named Salome. She was so provocative and alluring, that Pontius Pilate told her that he was so impressed that he would do any one thing she desired. Her answer was that she wanted the head of John the Baptist, under urging of her mother who was angry with John for almost drowning her during baptism. True to his word, he sent a soldier to the dungeon to bring back the head. This was accomplished promptly, but John was just the first of a long list of men who lost their heads to a beautiful dancer.

Paul, formerly Saul, continued his promotion of Jesus as the Son of God and the Savior of all people who believed in Him. Even though he lived seventy years after the death of Jesus, he traveled throughout the land in three journeys and accumulated thousands of frequent flyer miles. He eventually used these to go to the French Riviera where he lived out his life satisfied with a job well done. The religion prospered and grew and developed into one of the main promoters of stability and faith in the world.

CHAPTER FIVE

<u>COLUMBUS</u>

Christopher Columbus was born in 1451 to Dominico and Susannah Columbus at an early age in the town of Quinto, a suburb of Genoa in Italy. His father ran a wool shop in the bottom floor in a building with living quarters above. It was a dark, small building squeezed in between large establishments. As a child, he felt closed in the restricted area, and he could only dream of the wide-open spaces and distant horizons across the sea just outside of his home. Genoa, itself, was beautifully situated on the coast overlooking the most important deep-water protected harbor in the country. Mountains and forests that extended down to the water closely surrounded it. The narrow streets were where Christopher learned to walk and observe, but as a child he was not allowed to go out alone, because he had a very poor sense of direction and would probably get lost. His mother used to say of him; "He couldn't find his rattle in his crib." So he stayed in his house reading, learning Latin, mathematics and astronomy by himself. At other times while the other neighborhood boys were out tossing Frisbees to each other, or playing doctor with the little girls, Christopher would sit on a rock beside the sea dreaming of boats and far away resorts with fine hotels, floor shows, and casinos. When he saw foreign ships arriving from these distant cities and countries, it was natural for him to dream of the day when he would have his own ship and sail it to these distant ports.

Christopher's parent were aware of his sailing ambition, but his mother worried that with his poor sense of direction, he would be lost at sea and never find his way back.

Dominico's wool business flourished, and he opened a tavern that became a haven for sailors from all over the world. Here, Christopher heard the tales that increased his lust for travel. At age fifteen, his father bought him a small Chris-Craft but told him to stay inside the harbor. Of course he quickly lost his way, and he found himself out in the Aegean Sea. He saw an island that he thought was Genoa, but it turned out to be the island of Chios that was the gateway to the Orient, with busy market bustling with trade with merchants from the East. The island was beautiful, and Christopher promised himself he would return someday if he could find it again.

At this point in history, little was known about what was beyond the straight of Gibraltar or South of the northern cities of Africa. Christopher organized an exploration expedition to visit the Western Mediterranean as far as Portugal. He followed the shoreline to the Gibraltar Strait, and when he passed through it, he found himself in the Atlantic Ocean. He did not know where he was, but sailed into the island of St. Vincent. He went ashore with a few men and found a tavern where he was told that he was in Portugal. The men were hungry and tired, so he ordered some fried clams and Madeira wine to take out and returned to the ship.

The next day, Christopher and his men started their return home heading south toward Gibraltar and the entry to the Mediterranean Sea. After sailing for two days, they were attacked by ships from the French Navy. Columbus was surprise but had no means of defending himself and his ship was sunk. Luckily some Portuguese fisherman saw the plight of the Genoese sailors and rescued Columbus and most of his men.

When brought ashore, Columbus was told that the French suspected that he was a terrorist planning a surprise attack of France. Christopher told the Portuguese officials he was sailing toward Gibraltar on the way to Italy. That was when he realized he had been sailing North instead of South by mistake. He thanked his rescuers, and called King

John of Portugal on his cell phone and expressed his gratitude to Portugal for saving his party. The King was impressed by Columbus' sincerity and offered to send his party home on a cruise ship that happened to be going to Genoa. This established a firm relationship between Italy and Portugal that had future benefits.

When he returned home, Christopher was scolded by his mother for staying away so long and not calling. "Come on Ma, I was busy, and had too many things to do, but I thought of you every day." He gave her a nice blouse of Madeira cotton, which he had purchased at Macy's East, and she was pleased.

All the while he was dreaming of his experience in Portugal wondering what lay beyond the horizon, beyond the Atlantic Ocean. He had heard rumors and tales of a huge ledge at the end of the earth to the West that swallowed up ships that sailed too far. He knew that Newfoundland existed in a westerly direction, but was far to the north. What was sought of Newfoundland was unknown. When he pointed his radar toward the west, nothing showed up, but he intuitively felt that if he traveled far enough to the west he would come to China and India. He knew there was a great deal of trade with these far eastern countries with spices, silks, perfumes, marijuana, vodka and precious metals. The travel from that part of the world to Europe was very time consuming and fraught with danger by land and was even longer by water.

He thought if there were a western route by water, it would be shorter and safer. He also felt that the best place to start from would be Portugal. He arranged a meeting with King John and outlined his plan and the reasons for it. After much consideration, the King turned him down. However, Christopher did not give up and brought it up for consideration by Ferdinand and Isabella of Spain in 1486. These monarchs did not want to make their decisions themselves, and took the proposition before the Council of Scholars. Their progress was slow and was under consideration for two years.

During this period, Christopher met and fell in love with Beatriz DeArama who gave him peace of mind and physical pleasure while agonizing over the decision. Beatriz was a well-educated, twenty year old woman when she met Columbus in 1487. He was thirty-seven years old and becoming a myth for his Maritime genius and charm. They were in love with each other, but their romantic ventures were not always satisfactory. Because of his poor sense of direction, he could not always find what he was looking for. However, it must have been successful at least once, because in 1488 she gave birth to a son they named Ferdinand. They later had a legitimate son they named Diego. Columbus apparently favored Diego, and named him heir to his estate, leaving a small stipend for Beatriz.

He spent most of his time pleading his case for the expedition to the Far East by sailing west across the Atlantic. He was not very generous to Beatriz, and their relationship was faltering, but she lived until 1521, after Columbus' successful discovery of the new world.

Their were rumors about an affair between Christopher Columbus and Queen Isabella, but there was never any evidence or anything but a mutual admiration by the couple. However, one report that was widely circulated was that one night when Ferdinand was on a business trip to London, Isabella called Christopher over for a late visit. She waited impatiently, but he never arrived. He explained later that he couldn't find the palace.

When the Ottomans took over Turkey they closed off the Europe-Asia land route. The more adventurous sailors tried the route south of Africa and then north to the East Indies, Japan and China. This was very long and hazardous. The traders heard of the gold, silks and slave trade and the Portuguese explorers were anxious to try the western route. Columbus argued with the Portuguese King to sponsor this exploration, but the Council turned it down. Columbus was discouraged, so he turned to the Spanish monarchs. It took them several years to make up their minds, but eventually after hearing a program on History Channel describing the treasures and fine resorts in the islands of the Caribbean Sea, they gave Christopher the green light.

He started out with three ships, Santa Maria, Nina, and Pinta. He had ninety men to operate the three ships, leading the way on the Santa Maria. On August 3rd, 1492, they sailed west to the Canary Islands. From there he set the automatic pilot on a northwest course and expected to reach the East Indies in about three to four weeks. However, after six weeks with no sign of land, the crewmen became anxious about their safety.

Finally on October 12, they sighted an island that they named San Salvador, which is in the Bahamas. But Columbus thought he was at an island in the East Indies near Japan or China, so he called the inhabitants Indians. Thinking he was near the Asian mainland, he sailed into a harbor in the island of Cuba. He loaded his ships with cigars and sailed north to the island of Hispaniola which is now Haiti and the Dominican Republic. While_anchored offshore, a huge storm came up and the Santa Maria split apart on a reef. The men rescued the cigars and moved other essential equipment to the other ships and sailed for home, convinced he had found the west route to the East Indies. When he reported to Isabella and Ferdinand, he told them about the Indians and the lush tobacco fields and some unexplored gold mines. Before departing, Columbus left thirty-nine settlers and supplies in the name of Spain to explore the island and try to find the goldmine that he knew was in the vicinity. He felt they would have the cooperation of the native men and women, because they had established a favorable attitude.

The Spanish monarchs were eager to exploit the new find and sponsored a fleet of seventeen ships and fourteen hundred men. They left Spain on September 25, 1493 and reached Hispaniola in six weeks after a short stop in Puerto Rico for a few days at the El San Juan. After leaving a small contribution at the casino, they sailed to Haiti. The natives were very friendly, and the women were beautiful. They also proved that they welcomed the companionship of the men. The inhabitants of the island had never been exposed to European diseases and had never developed resistance to new infections. As a result, they succumbed to simple diseases like mumps, measles, and chicken pox. The native girls returned the favor by giving the men syphilis that was endemic to the area. The sailors brought back this disease to Europe along with some gold.

The third voyage departed Spain, May 30, 1498 with six ships intending to claim Hispaniola for Spain and explore its gold mines and rum factories.

However, with his poor sense of direction, he found himself far south of his destination at the island of Trinidad off the coast of Venezuela. As he sailed along the north coarse, he finally realized he was not in the East Indies but had discovered a whole new great continent. He then proceeded north to Hispaniola where he named the capital city Santo Domingo. He was disappointed to find that half of the men who had been left there on the previous trip were dead, apparently by violence among themselves. He also noted that many of the young native women had developed enlarged, rounded, protrurences of their abdomens.

The fourth and last trip, sponsored by Ferdinand and Isabella, was again meant to find a westward route to the Far East. On May 9, 1502. He set sail with four ships from Cadiz, Spain. His automatic pilot took him due west. His ships were battered by a severe storm, which had not been reported by the weather bureau. He became very sick and while throwing up over the rail, he lost a gold watch that had been given to him by Queen Isabella.

When the storm had subsided, he continued west until they reached what are now Honduras, Costa Rica and Panama. At the narrowest part of Panama, he heard that just a few miles west was a great body of water, but he was too tires, exhausted and had malaria. On the way home the ship was badly battered and Columbus was too sick to continue, so they stopped at Jamaica and with a good supply of rum and conch chowder he slowly recovered, but it was a year he was able to resume the homeward trip. Alas, the ordeal had taken too much out of him, and he died on May 20,1506. In his will he expressed a desire to be buried in Hispaniola, but the ship carrying his body got lost and he was buried in Ohio.

CHAPTER SIX
<u>GEORGE WASHINGTON</u>

John Washington, the grandfather of Gustav, left England in 1657 to come to America. He married the daughter of a tobacco planter who had a very successful plantation. Tobacco was the way to get rich quickly, because the demand in England and in the colonies was rapidly growing. John's son Lawrence followed his father in buying more and more land. He married a woman, the daughter of another plantation owner, increasing their land and fortunes. The family prospered as Virginia grew and members of the family became important members of the community as Justices of Peace, Church Wardens, and Legislator Members. Lawrence's son, Augustine, known as "Gus", also planted tobacco and ran an iron works factory. He married Jane Butler and started a family including two sons, Lawrence Jr. and Augustine Jr. In May 1730, Jane died leaving Gus with two sons and a business. This was too much for him to handle alone, so in 1731 he married Mary Bell, a twenty-three year old planter's daughter. She could hardly write her name, but she brought more money into the family and was a robust athletic horsewoman.

Their first child was George. Within six years since they had plenty of time and money, they had four other children. These were private people and had little part in George's career. Mary was tough, bossy, smoked a corn-cobbed pipe and showed no love for her children, other than having them. George had no love for her either, but showed respect for her as his mother. Even after he was grown and married he never invited Mary to his home or introduced her to his wife. In 1738, Gus moved his family to Ferry

Farm near Fredericksburg, Virginia where he owned 1750 acres of land.

George had very little if any formal schooling but learned to read and write on his own. He was very good with numbers, arithmetic, geography and history. He studied and learned about civility, behavior in company and wrote essays teaching youngsters about manners and morality. George admired his half-brother Lawrence who practiced these rules of behavior at all times. Lawrence was an officer in the Virginia Militia and he was a devoted and skillful reader and set a very good example for younger brother George who admired and copied his example.

As a youngster, George was always well behaved, polite and considerate of other people, mostly because of his older brother's influence.

However, Lawrence became seriously ill with tuberculosis and left George mostly on his own. At age thirteen, George became friendly with the sons of some of the farmhands who had little schooling and were frequently apprehended for minor infractions, such as car theft, and property damage. George joined them at first reluctantly in writing graffiti and horse and carriage theft. It became their pastime to go around chopping down trees on the property of the more wealthy citizens. They would chop down a cherry tree and just leave it on the ground and run away. George saw this as a waste, but instead of trying to stop them, he said "This cherry wood is beautiful and strong, why not use it for some good purpose?" One of his "friends" had a table saw in his basement and the boys began cutting the wood for various useful purposes. George with his manual and imaginative qualities knew that Fairfax County and that area of Virginia were the fastest growing parts of the country. He reasoned that there would be a rapid growth in home building and each home would need kitchen cabinets. Cherry wood would make wonderful cabinets with their richly polished shine and durability. His companions agreed to the feasibility of the idea, and immediately set about to cut down cherry trees in the thick forests as fast as possible. They took the trees from the depth of the woods to avoid detection. They made some sample cabinets, and contracted with the builders who were constructing the new homes. They were uniformly impressed with the adaptability and beauty of the cabinets and began ordering them in large quantities. One saw was not nearly enough to keep up with the demand, so George, whose family had a wonderful reputation in Virginia consulted a banker who was overjoyed to finance the business. They bought an old stable and five more saws and hired four more poor boys that were delighted for the opportunity to work for money. The supply of cherry wood seemed endless, and they became skillful in carpentry under George's tutelage and produced hundreds of kitchen cabinets which were so beautifully made they helped the builders sell streets full of houses with beautiful expensive kitchens.

The boys named their company Virginia Kitchens, Inc., and were promptly accepted for trading in the Virginia Stock Exchange, and it became the first IPO of the New World. None of the Washington family was interested in stock investing, so George's father was totally ignorant of what was going on. One morning, he awoke and noted that one of his cherry trees had been chopped down. He reluctantly took George outside and asked him if he knew who had chopped down the tree. George laughed, and said "Come on Dad, get with it." "Don't you read anything but the Christian Science Monitor? "I'm the CEO of the fastest growing business in Virginia." He told his father about the cherry tree cabinet business from the start to the IPO. His father listened and didn't know whether to be angry, proud, skeptical or delighted that his son had the wisdom to develop a prank into a large business. His first question after gaining his composure was "Are you making enough money to pay back your debts, and do you think this is going to continue?" George responded, "Dad, are you kidding?" "Don't you know that would be insider information?" "Do you want to go to jail like Mr. Gay or that bakery woman?" His father dropped the subject knowing that George was a minor and he would be in charge of George's finances until he was eighteen. So he set about helping his son run the business in conjunction with his ongoing tobacco business. They renamed the business "Washington's Smoking Cabinets."

In 1752, George's brother, Lawrence, died of tuberculosis at Mt. Vernon with George at his bedside. Lawrence's wife, Ann, held the Mt. Vernon Estate in trust for infant Sarah, but George visited frequently.

George wanted a commission in the British Army. Commissions were not granted as a result of good work as a soldier, but they were purchased, and George was unable to afford it. Ann died in 1760 leaving Mt. Vernon to George. At that time, the French occupied Southern Canada. Their main interest in this area was in furs. The British occupied the area south of Canada and was occupied by the Indians. In 1775, General Edward Braddock landed in Virginia leading a contingent of fifteen hundred British soldiers. George knew the area well and offered his services as an unpaid volunteer. Braddock had heard about George's bravery and knowledge of the territory and offered him a place on his personal staff. England and France both wanted this area for different reasons. The French were interested only in Canadian furs, while the English wanted the land as an extension of their Colonial occupation. However, the only real occupants were Indians who had settled all the way down New York to Pennsylvania. They were not ready to give up their land to the French. By this time, Braddock had made George Washington a Lieutenant colonel, and he became friendly with Queen Aliquippa who was the wife of one of the Indian Chiefs. George had become friendly with the Queen, and the two of them were on a scouting exploration of the area, when a sudden and unexpected storm forced them to spend a night in a cave. They were cut off from their combined Indian-Virginian forces that had been fighting the French. There was a small fire in the cave, and they could only keep from freezing by sharing body heat. They survived the night and the next morning, when the storm m had passed, they made their way to an improvised fortress where their co-fighters were anxiously awaiting them. Somehow, after this, the Indian-Virginia combined forces were able to subdue their French adversaries even though they were vastly outnumbered, but through a series of tactical mistakes, which canceled themselves out, Colonel Washington became a national hero.

He returned to Williamsburg where he became a much sought after bachelor by all the available (and not so available) ladies at the numerous balls and other social functions. He was tall and straight, young and well muscled, and good looking except for some defective teeth. His demeanor was composed and dignified and he was considerate and wealthy. With all these attributes, it is not surprising that Colonel Washington did not lack for female companionship, and his compatibility was the talk of the community. It was during this period that he became known as "The Father of the Country." His only physical drawback was the condition of his teeth. This interfered with his social life to the extent that he sought the help of a New England part time dentist named Paul Revere. He visited his office on Beacon St., in Boston, where Revere planned extensive dental surgery including extraction's, two root canals and a bridge of wooden teeth. This set George back four thousand dollars, but they did improve his appearance, although they still made a "clacking" sound when he spoke. Some of his female friends found splinters in their mouth after an evening's entertainment.

Among the eligible ladies, was Martha Custis, widow of Daniel Park Custis, and the richest unmarried lady in all Virginia. She also was twenty-four years old, pretty and charming. George called on Martha and stayed overnight occasionally in order to play with Martha's children, John and Martha Custis. A series of such engagements followed and the children were joyously impressed by the attention of the tall, straight, playful young officer, but were unhappy about being put to bed at an early hour.

On the occasion of his last visit, before being ordered to the command of his regiment at Fort Henry where the French were pushing the British back toward Lake Champlain, he bought her a beautiful diamond ring he had purchased at Bloomingdale's. She recognized this as an indication of George's love, and knew in her heart he would return to her.

When George arrived at the battle area, he was surprised and angry that he was not recognized as a full colonel in the British Army, because he led only a small Virginia company. He and his men fought valiantly and effectively and repulsed the French adversaries. When the battle was over George resigned his commission and returned home depressed and frustrated. However, he finally accepted his situation, married Martha and set about refurbishing the mansion at Mt. Vernon. He and Martha drove around the Virginia countryside in her Studebaker, spent weekends at Williamsburg Inn, joined the Fairfax Country Club, and played golf three times a week, followed by a couple of daiquiris and light chatter with the female members. Saturday nights they frequently went for dinner at the Fredericksburg Ritz and danced to the music of Marquis Goodman.

Everything was well for a year, but then things began to change. Some of the slaves died of Aids, the tobacco industry that was their main source of income, was hit by some damaging lawsuits and the tobacco stocks tumbled. Virginia was growing, meaning more children, more schools and higher taxes. George thought about going back into the kitchen cabinet business, but the cherry trees had been hit by a serious blight and pine was hard to work with and was less attractive. George still had enough for some modest gambling, duck hunting and occasional horse racing. He was an avid reader and subscribed to New Yorker, Reader's Digest and Playboy.

Washington was not a religious man. He was not a follower of other people's beliefs, but he felt that some other power made most decisions in the long run, but he still felt obligated to do what he felt was right. Washington's retirement from political and military service did not hinder his feeling of loyalty to Great Britain. However, the passage of the "Stamp Act" in 1765 and the Townsend Act in 1767 which imposed duties on imports to be collected in America by royal officials. George realized Colonial production of manufactured and farm products would deteriorate. The Virginia Assembly joined the other colonies in violent protests, but George was slow to acknowledge the coming financial crisis.

In 1774, he heard of the Boston Tea Party to which he was not invited. Instead, he invited the representatives of the other colonies to a tea party of his own at Mt. Vernon. After tea and cookies, they discussed the proposals for retaliation, and cooperation with Boston for resistance to the British reprisals which were sure to come. The result of this party was the decision to attend a congressional meeting in Philadelphia to discuss the main issues. George attended the meeting, but not as an official representative of Virginia. He knew his speech making was limited, but he was socially active with the other representatives. He played cards, dined out frequently, visited local taverns and discussed some important questions with some ladies of the night. However, he found time to mingle with the elected representatives from the other colonies. From the learned of the devastation being caused by Britain's policies. They remembered George Washington's military career in the French and Indian wars and assessed him on his youthful, easy and soldier-like demeanor. He showed extreme interest in Boston's plight and offered to arm and personally lead one thousand men at his own expense for the relief of Boston.

After returning to Mt. Vernon, the militia voted him to be their field officer and if combat occurred, he would command all Virginia's forces.

On April 27, George Washington received word of bloody fighting in Massachusetts at Concord and Lexington. On May 4, George packed his SUV with clean clothes, a few cases of whiskey, some bagels and cheese, told Martha he left her some grocery money in the sugar bowl, gave her a pat on the ass and was off.

As he drove along the Virginia roads crowds of people lined the roadway, cheering and waving to their hero. As he approached Philadelphia, a marching band and a tickertape parade greeted him. In a bill passed in Congress, on June 15, 1775, George Washington was appointed general of all the continental forces. In accepting the office, Washington stated he did not consider himself capable of undertaking such an important assignment, but since Congress voted unanimously for his appointment, he would humbly accept the office.

George knew he was in good physical condition, because he had spent much of his early retirement time throwing money across the Potomac River and swimming across to retrieve it.

When he undertook his duties, he reviewed the combats in New England starting with Concord and Lexington. He was very impressed with the determination and ferocity of the New Englanders' resistance to the organized British soldiers. However, other segments of his army were untried, and he worried about their determination. He soon had the opportunity to test them.

He learned from a spy satellite that the English had hired a regiment of Hessian professionals to reclaim Trenton in southern New Jersey and then Philadelphia. Washington's army was west of the Delaware River, moving to cut off an enemy attack. It was December and it was extremely cold as he moved his men along the west bank of the river until he was directly opposite the Hessian troops. He moved at night and remained unobserved by the enemy. On Christmas Eve, there was a very heavy snowstorm, and Washington didn't think the Hessians would be expecting a late night attack. They were relaxing and warming themselves with holiday spirit while across the Delaware River, Washington loaded twenty four hundred men in large cargo boats and began rowing across. It was snowing heavily and ice was forming on the river, but Washington had provided all his men with warm fur underwear and fur caps with earmuffs. They silently crossed to the other shore and pounced on the sleeping Germans. Many of the enemy soldiers were killed, nine hundred prisoners were taken and much arms and supplies were captured. Washington was pleased with the conduct of his men under horrible conditions and he held a victory meeting expressing his praise and thanks for their effort.

Shortly thereafter Lord Cornwallis was making a march on New York, but he ran into Washington's Army unexpectedly and was beaten off by a determined effort and support from some "smart bombs", from Princeton College. This battle was the start of the end of the British invasion of the new land. Washington wanted to mop up scattered remnants of enemy forces in the Maryland, Virginia area.

The French had shown a desire to aid the colonists, mainly for financial reasons but also to damage the chances of their enemy Great Britain, from securing an establishment in America. Lord Cornwallis had moved a contingent of his soldiers to the Chesapeake Bay, Yorktown area. There they were surrounded by French and Colonial forces and were thoroughly overwhelmed. Many British soldiers were killed or captured in a battle that determined the virtual end of the war. Cornwallis surrendered to Washington reluctantly and still maintained a small compliment of soldiers in New York, but they had been unarmed and awaited transportation back to New England. General Washington's stature had risen higher than ever by his bravery and leadership. However, the continental treasury had been depleted by the war, and the government owed thousands of dollars to the soldiers for pay as well as merchants for war materials. The soldiers who had fought bravely for their independence were angry, as were the business people who had lent money and materials to the government. The Commander in Chief addressed a meeting of discontented citizens who for the first time showed disappointment and anger. However, in his gentle and persuasive manner, he explained that they had his gratitude and love and he would do everything he could to se that all debts were paid. He was sympathetic and forthright enough so that they ended up cheering him. When the last of the British Army had left New York, George addressed the remaining soldiers, thanked them again and they were free to return home.

George's old SUV was beaten and old and he wasn't sure that he could make the trip from New York to Mt. Vernon, so he bought a one-way ticket on Continental Airlines. He called ahead to Martha on his cell phone to pick him up at the airport at 5:00pm. When he arrived they greeted each other with hugs and kisses and they stopped at the Fairfax Deli for pastrami on whole wheat while she had a bowl of oxtail soup. As they were driving home, she asked him "What's new?" He replied, "Not much, we just got King George off our backs." Martha responded, "That's nice, what are you going to do now?" He told Martha that unless she had found some way to make money they were now seventy five hundred dollars in debt. She took that news bravely and after a few minutes she said that there were always crowds of people coming to look at their home in Mt. Vernon. She said people knew that the leader of the Colonial Army lived there, and they wanted to see his home. He said he hoped there were no single men. She laughed and said, "Only couples, and no one stayed overnight." She confided that she charged fifty cents a head for a tour and had accumulated a little money. "Now that you're home probably we could open a little gift shop." He said he would consider that, but soon his time might be limited because it's possible that he might become the President of the new United States, Martha thought that might be very nice if it didn't interfere with their home life too much.

Delegates from the thirteen colonies were summoned to Philadelphia in May 1787, to formulate a constitution uniting all the colonies now called "states into a single country giving each state its own sovereignty in local issues but subject to the dictates of the whole country as decided by Congress. It took weeks for the delegates to work out all the details of The Bill of Rights which spelled out the rights of freedom of religion, speech, press, to cheat on taxes, and deceive stock holders. The individual states had already elected Senators and Representatives. At the end of the conflict with England, Washington had announced his retirement from public and military service. During the weeks of consideration of appointing a President, the members of Congress could present no other candidate than

George Washington who had done no campaigning or public appearances or any indication that he might be interested in the office. On April 14, he was notified of his unanimous election by the delegates. He was emotionally overwhelmed by the honor and actually doubted his qualifications to lead a new country out of the chaotic conditions he saw forthcoming. However, the citizens had no such doubts, and when the announcement of his election was made there was jubilation, cheering and public celebration. The acceptance by the people was so exuberant, he did not have the heart to refuse. Even Martha was so overwhelmed by her husband's popularity, she closed the gift shop at Mt. Vernon and spent the next two weeks shopping for new clothes at Wallmarts, using the new credit cards which were gladly issued to the wife of the new President. George had settled his headquarters in New York City because of its' central location, but Philadelphia had remained the capital of the country. Martha moved into a house in New York and was able to attend the inaugural balls and parties in both cities and was universally accepted by society. However, all the activities soon began to wear her down and she longed to return to her home in Virginia. George remained mostly in New York but returned home frequently to make sure his wife was happy and well taken care of.

The financial state of the country was abysmal, but the President was adamant about paying the former soldiers what was owed to them. The country was divided even at that time between the business oriented North and the agrarian South.

Alexander Hamilton was appointed Secretary of the Treasury. He was successful in inducing businessmen both local and foreign to invest in industrial enterprises in the North while tobacco and cotton farms flourished in the South. As time went by, the United States gradually pulled together but always separated by North-South differences. Economy could not keep up with expenses, friction with native Indians, French and English and there were rumors and accusations of dishonesty among party leaders. The

President was in the middle of all those situations but always felt out of place in dealing with economic problems.

He served two terms and near the conclusion, the new Federalist Party tried to convince him to run again, but he was too old, and too tired to consider it. He had made thousands of friends and admirers but also the ire of the southern planters for his anti-slavery campaign that never came to fruition. After his retirement to Mt. Vernon he tried to remain a private citizen with Martha and his secretary. They never re-opened the gift shop, and in December 1,1797, while still worrying about slavery he became seriously ill and quietly expired with his loving Martha by his side.

George Washington was probably the most loved and respected President the country ever had with the possible exception of Richard Nixon. As we have seen, he was industrious and innovative even as a youngster. He was laid-back and rarely showed much emotion, except when discussing slavery and inequality in the status of citizenship. He was true to his friends and relentless in dealing with opponents. As the first President he set valuable policies for his successors to emulate. He was liberal but discreet in his private life but had deep respect and love for his wife Martha. He was truly "The Father of his Country."

CHAPTER SEVEN
ABRAHAM LINCOLN

Abraham Lincoln's father Thomas was a descendant of Samuel Lincoln who emigrated in 1637 from Hingham, England to Hingham, MA. Thomas was an uneducated farmhand, but later developed skill at woodworking, and earned a living as a carpenter. In 1806, at twenty-eight years of age, Thomas married Nancy Hanks. Thomas and Nancy lived on a farm in Elizabethtown, Kentucky where Abraham was born February 12, 1809. A sister, Sarah, had been born there two years earlier in 1807. The children went to a log schoolhouse where they learned reading, writing, calculus and electronics.

Farming was difficult, and it was impossible to operate a farm at that time without slave help of which Thomas did not approve. Consequently he decided to move his family to Indiana. The Lincoln's loaded their sparse possessions into their jeep and traveled north to Indiana. The Lincolns found life in Indiana harder than in Kentucky. Thomas tried to convert 160 acres of forest into a farm. Thom and Abraham set out to build a log cabin. Although he was young, Abraham was large for his age, and had enough strength to swing an ax. He was a great help to his father, and the family moved into it in February 1817.

Life was a little easier for them, but the local Indians resented their intrusion into their land and constantly threatened them with poison gas. Thomas and Abraham sealed the doors and windows with duck tape, but unfortunately one morning Thomas awoke and found his wife Nancy dead of asphyxiation. She was buried among the trees near the cabin.

Life on the farm became dull and depressing without Nancy, so they decided to return to Kentucky. Thomas had exchanged the Jeep for a Ford 4x4 in which they packed their belongings. The trip to Kentucky was uneventful, and they settled in a rural area near Louisville.

In 1819, Thomas met and married Sarah Johnston, a widow with three children. This ended the period of loneliness, but Abraham wasn't impressed with his new relatives. He began taking long walks around the outskirts of Louisville when he wasn't reading and educating himself and studying history on History Channel.com. His parents joined the local Baptist Church, but Abraham never joined any church but had deeply religious feelings and knew the Bible thoroughly. Later, while President, he often opened it for comfort and guidance.

On one of his walks around Louisville, he came upon a beautiful huge farm enclosed by a handsome white wooden fence. He was very impressed and wondered what was grown there. When he walked around to the front entrance, he saw a large sign that said "Calamity Farm." He walked to a remote section where there were no signs of people, and climbed over the fence. He was surprised to see that there was no sign of growing products, but there were dozens of beautiful horses grazing there. They were the most handsome animals he had ever seen. They were large, small, bay, chestnut, gray but all graceful and well groomed. There were immaculate barns with bales of hay and buckets of water. He saw some of the caretakers who observed him, but seeing that he was a young, interested person, they didn't question his presence.

On one occasion, while roaming around the farm, he came upon a large barn with a sign "Breeding Shed." He had no idea what that meant, but he was tall enough to look into a window. When he did so, he almost fell over backward at what he saw. It was a most amazing sight to him. He saw several men holding a horse in place with ropes and hands. Some other men led in another horse behind the first one and he was overwhelmed by the size of the instrument being helped into position. When the event was finished, Abraham couldn't wait to tell his father what he had observed. Thomas listened as his son described the whole procedure. When he was finished, his father told him "That's what life is about." "To maintain the preservation of any species a male and female unite to produce an offspring, whether it is a human, animal, or even an insect." "Eleven months from now, that female horse will give birth to a baby horse which will eventually grow up and produce more horses." He told Abraham that Calamity Farm was the largest and most successful racehorse breeding farm in the world and has produced many championship horses. Abraham said he was amazed by the size of the horses' baby producer. He was ashamed of his own, but Thomas told him not to worry, he had enough to produce many offspring. That comforted the boy, but he still felt overwhelmed.

Abraham continued to walk and explore the farm, until one day he discovered a whole fenced in farm that was growing a bush-like plant that did not appear to produce any fruit or vegetable. He figured it was growing some sort of feed for the horses. He noticed a number of people he had never seen, walking through the fields, occasionally picking some and filling bags with it, and leaving through the rear gate and filling their trucks.

To his astonishment, he noticed one of the men, stopped, rolled up a few of the leaves and smoked them. On further observation, he noticed other men doing the same thing. He thought they must have been testing the plants purity or effectiveness. His curiosity was aroused, so one day when no one was around, he picked some leaves, rolled them up, and lit them. He took a few deep breaths and started choking. After a few minutes the coughing stopped, and he noticed a strange feeling of serenity, but familiar objects appeared strange to him, and a feeling of euphoria came over him.

When he came back to earth, he realized why "Calamity Farm' horses ran so well-they were always very happy. Later, when he told his father of his experiment, Thomas told him smoking of anything, even tobacco, was unhealthy and dangerous, and he should never do it again.

A few years later, Thomas was dissatisfied with life in Kentucky, especially his old distaste for slavery. He moved the family west. At the time Abraham was twenty-one years old. He was six feet, four inches and muscular from his years of chopping wood and hard work. Even as a young boy, he had shown ability as a speaker. He could do imitations and invent stories, and he had the ability to communicate with all people. He ended up in New Salem, Illinois, twenty miles west of Springfield.

He had no trouble finding work, but very frequently while walking the streets of the town, he became acquainted with many people. With his six foot four inch muscular build and his easy way of speaking to people, he became well known and had many friends. He was often surprised when strange, well-dressed men approached him and offered free scholarships to a number of the large schools in the area. He was never interested in formal education and refused the offers. One gentleman who approached him was more persistent and made more specific offers. He would pay no tuition, he would have free room and board, books and transportation would be free, and he wouldn't have to attend classes if he didn't want to. Abraham was suspicious of such an offer and asked, "What's the catch?" "No catch," was the reply, you would just play basketball."

Abraham didn't know a basketball from a coconut, but he offered think about it. In considering it, he thought that since he had no real education, had not traveled, didn't know any prominent people, and had no real qualification, he should probably go into politics. He knew that all politicians were lawyers, so this basketball scholarship could lead to a law degree.

Accordingly, he contacted the representative of None such State University, and told him he would accept the offer, but he would need new clothes for school. The admissions officer greeted Abraham, made all his living requirements, and bought him a whole new wardrobe. At first he was overwhelmed by the size of the school and the number of students. It took him a while to become acclimated, but with his powerful appearance and gentle manner he rapidly made friends and became very popular. When it came time for the first basketball practice, he was given a uniform of a shirt with a large "N" on it and a pair of purple shorts. He looked strange, with his long, thin legs and powerful chest and arms. The rules of the game were explained to him, and he was told that to be a good basketball player, it was necessary to be fast and powerful and "don't let the opposing players push you around." It took time for him to learn about passing the ball and dribbling. When he had developed a little skill in these departments, he began dribbling down the court, and if any other player was in his way, he would charge into him, full speed, and there would be a great collision with the other player flying off the court.

After three practice sessions, all but three of the players were disabled, in casts or on crutches. In spite of warnings and admonitions by the coach, Abe could not contain his aggressiveness.

He always apologized when he injured anyone and expressed regrets. But finally the coach, in fear of losing his whole team, and his job, invited Abraham to resign from the team, but in fairness, the school would live up to its promise and he could continue on with his law education.

After two years of law study, Abraham felt he knew enough to go into practice. He met and married Mary Todd and eventually had four sons. The marriage was not without differences, usually based on Mary's treatment of people as her slaves, and her husbands' abhorrence of slavery that she condoned.

In 1832, Lincoln ran for State Legislature, but was defeated. However, two years later he ran again and was elected. He was admitted to the bar in 1837. However, after some personal and professional setbacks, he retired from the legislature.

In 1846, he was elected to Congress and served until 1849. At that time, Lincoln had lost a son, and was discouraged about the state of the government and retired from political life, but he was regarded by political people as honest, capable, but a self developed small town politician, but a lucid thinker and a clever man before a crowd.

After he retired, he went back to the practice of law. He won a few small tort cases, and spent several months on the legal circuit in central Illinois. He turned down several proposals to run for office in the Whig party. He turned these down, but he appeared as speaker for other candidates on numerous occasions as long as they opposed slavery. He quickly became recognized as a thoughtful and talented speaker. He had a manner that captivated and entranced an audience.

He was not satisfied with the practice of law, and after losing an important case against Microsoft, he decided he would be more suited for politics than law. Consequently in 1860, Abraham Lincoln ran for the presidency of the United States and was elected by a wide margin. He was inaugurated on March 4, 1861.

In the months before the election, many southern states threatened to withdraw from the Union if Lincoln were elected because of his opposition to slavery. After the election, South Carolina passed an ordinance declaring the Union dissolved. Ten other southern states joined South Carolina, organizing the "Confederate States of America." On April 12, 1861, the Confederates fired upon Fort Sumter in Charleston harbor and the Civil War was started. With the confederate capital in Richmond, Virginia, the Union command thought it would be easy to march right in and overpower the rebels. The rift between the North and South was not only about slavery, but also about the economic and philosophical differences between the two sections of the country. The South was agrarian oriented while the North was involved with commerce and manufacturing. Of course the southern farmers could not function profitably without the slaves. Consequently, the southern legislators decided to secede from the United States, and continue their farming with slave labor.

When Abraham Lincoln was inaugurated, he vowed that he would not allow the United States to become divided. Two days after the fall of Fort Sumter, Lincoln placed an ad in the New York Times for volunteers to uphold the Union. The North sent more volunteers than the government could equip. Seventy five thousand soldiers assembled in Washington. An equal number of Confederates took position across the Potomac River in Virginia. The Northerners clambered for action, and when satellite observation showed no evidence of weapons of mass destruction, President Lincoln ordered General Irving McDowell to march on Richmond. This resulted in the first battle of Bull Run. On July 21, the Confederate forces defeated the Union troops.

Then the President realized the war was going to be a long one. He then turned command over to General George McClellan. McClellan trained the soldiers and officers and finally moved against Bull Run (also called Manassas), and in the battle on August 29, and 30, 1862, the Union forces were defeated again, mainly through the brilliant direction of Confederate General, "Stonewall Jackson." Lincoln was furious when he saw the way the battle was going while watching it on CNN. After the defeat, he called McClellan back with his forces to regroup and be prepared to defend Washington.

On September 17, 1962, under Lincoln's prodding, McClellan and his men defeated the army of Robert E. Lee in the bloody battle of Antietam. However, McClellan failed to follow up his advantage, making one excuse after another. This delay allowed Lee to escape to the north. Lincoln was so disgusted that he discharged McClellan and eventually placed the Union Army under the direction of General George Meade.

By means of intelligence infiltrates and spy planes, Meade learned that Lee was preparing to move north, slightly inland, preparing to attack New York City. Meade then moved his troops along a shoreline route going north, and moving rapidly by means of fast trains and transport planes, surrounded and surprised Lee in the town of Gettysburg, Pennsylvania on July 1, 1863. The battle was furious and lasted three days, but with the aid of armored vehicles and gatlin machine guns, the Union forces defeated Lee's army. However, Meade, following McClellan's mistake, failed to press his advantage and allowed the combatants to retreat all the way down to Maryland.

The President again was furious with his general and sent him an E-mail berating him for his ineptitude and ordered him to return to Washington immediately. He also instructed Secretary of State Howell to issue a statement that General Meade broke off the battle when the enemy was defeated, because too many civilians were being killed or injured, and we were inciting the wrath of France.

At the dedication of the cemetery at Gettysburg, Lincoln delivered the Gettysburg Address that has become one of the highlights of his career. He demoted General Meade and appointed a hard driving, hard drinking, cigar smoking, Ulysses S. Grant to take command of the Union Army. Lincoln had heard about Grant on a program he heard on History Channel. When he brought Grant to Washington for an interview, Lincoln was convinced he had made the right choice.

Almost immediately the tide of the war changed, and the Union army was victorious in the Shenandoah Valley, the Wilderness, Spotsylvania, and Cold Harbor in the spring and summer of 1864. By this time the Confederate Army was decimated, exhausted and running out of supplies. They called upon France, Russia and Rangoon for help, but they all knew the Confederates had no chance, so they refused.

President Lincoln was glued to CNN during this period and was delighted with Fox Blister's reports of the battle in progress. Lincoln had been re-elected after some dubious reactions following the 1863 defeats, but when the tide turned his victory was assured. On April 9, 1865, Lee surrendered to Grant at Appomattox, and the war ended. Of course the President was overjoyed with the cessation of the conflict and the preservation of the united country.

On the evening of April 14, 1865, Abraham and Mary Lincoln attended a performance at Ford's Theater in Washington. They were seated in a private box, when a single shot from the gun of a well-known local actor John Wilkes Booth mortally wounded him. Later Booth, along with some other conspirators was shot and killed. In the meantime, Lincoln was unconscious and bleeding from a wound in his head. He was carried to a house across the street where he died eight hours later.

He is considered one of the greatest American presidents and was loved and respected for his rise from an uneducated farm boy to the highest political office in the world.

CHAPTER EIGHT
<u>EINSTEIN</u>

Albert Einstein was born on March 14, 1879 in Ulm, in Germany to Hermann and Pauline. In the next year they moved to Munich. He had a younger sister named Maria. When he was an infant, he was very slow to learn, and his parents were afraid he was going to be backward. As he grew a little older, he seemed withdrawn and uninterested in his surroundings. He wasn't interested in Sesame Street or Mickey Mouse, and he didn't learn to speak until he was twelve years old. His first words were, "Gravity keeps the whole world together." From that, his mother knew that he must be stupid, but at least he could talk.

Soon after that, he had occasion to see a compass, and he was intrigued by the fact that the needle always pointed in one direction. From that, he deduced there must be some invisible force acting on the needle. He was so impressed by this possibility that he came out of his private shell and began questioning other natural events which other people took for granted, such as why does water always run down hill, why doesn't the moon fall down, and what is the real difference between living and dead? The fascination with natural phenomena governed his thoughts and activities for the rest of his life. He never bothered with the pastimes of the other boys his age. He didn't know any players' batting average, and he had no idea who was Green Bay's quarterback. This made him a "loner," and older people thought he was missing some cards from his deck.

He hated the compulsory process of regimentation in schools and of course did poorly in school except for

Mathematics. He took violin lessons from at six to fourteen. He did not like the disciplined lessons, and practice sessions, but for some reason he fell in love with Cole Porter and Richard Rodgers and played their tunes constantly. Throughout his life whenever he was depressed or discouraged, he turned to music for comfort. For this he did not need company, and rarely established close or prolonged personal relationships. Strangely, he developed a passionate interest in social justice and inter-personal responsibility. This aroused in him an interest in photography and a curiosity in understanding why people do what they do, just as he tried to figure why natural events occur as they do.

Although Einstein was born and brought up as a Jew, he never became "religious" as far as belief in the customs of Judaism, but he felt inwardly that there must have been some force to establish and organize the order of the world.

When he was fifteen, his family moved to Milan, but Albert chose to remain in Munich to finish his schooling, which amounted mostly to Mathematics and Philosophy. As soon as he received his certificate, he saw that Germany was being taken over by dominating, antisocial influences, and patriotism was merely another reason for senseless murder. Consequently, he took his violin and his certificates and boarded the train to Milan. In the Italian atmosphere he felt released from the German oppression and regimentation.

After a period of rest, he wanted to return to the world of Mathematics and Geometry. The two men he most respected lived in Germany, but he refused to go back again, so he moved to Zurich, between Italy and Germany and he became a Swiss citizen. He applied for admission to the Swiss Federal Institute of Technology where he was accepted immediately. Here he found a new liberal attitude of teachers without the rote and forced learning which had alienated him in Germany. He admired his teachers and developed personal relationships with them. In turn, they were impressed with Albert's knowledge of Math and

Physics and also his healthy skepticism of accepted scientific principals.

Through the computer that came with his room, he met a pretty, dark haired Hungarian girl in the chat room. They communicated by E- mail, and he found out her name was Mileva and she was as devoted to science as he was. They eventually met and found that they shared more than a scholastic interest. In order to pay her expenses, she danced in a local bistro and displayed considerable talent. They studied together, sometimes dined out together, and engaged in mutual research of deep problems.

Albert's reputation for his analytic and original approach to scientific and mathematical study impressed the faculty, and he was appointed Assistant Professor, which was a great honor for a young man of eighteen. However, the pay was poor and the work was time consuming. His knowledge of calculus, trigonometry and geometry were becoming legend in the scientific world. However, one evening when dining out with Meliva, he questioned the bill. It was a small amount for the two people, but it puzzled him and he spoke to the manager. He thought it was correct, so Albert showed it to Mileva who could not find an error. It turned out that Albert Einstein was unable to add. Apparently, addition was not important in advanced mathematics, but it caused some problems in his later life. When he was making enough money to open a checking account, his balance was always a mess. As a result, he was constantly overdrawn, and his creditors had him in small claims court frequently. He realized he couldn't add, so he decided to buy a computer to do his figuring. He purchased a new computer with up to date Microsoft software. However, he could never learn to use it for anything but chat room and mail.

The first time he was required to file an income tax report, he filled it out himself, but in three weeks it was returned to him, and across the top, was "HUH?" From then on, he had an accountant do his figuring.

The years between 1900-1905 were significant growth years for Albert. He became a Swiss citizen. The scientific world was making remarkable progress with the discovery of electricity and magnetism, and the electron theory. There was beginning to be interest shown in the atom, and the electric-magnetic field. He heard about Benjamin Franklin's experiments, but he could not understand how anyone could be stupid enough to go out into a field and fly a kite during an electrical storm.

In the early 1900's he wrote a paper on "capillary" and another on "Brownian Movement," both being published in scientific journals. All the time, he was continuing his study and speculation into the molecular theory and the atomic structure of matter.

In October 1902, Einstein suffered the greatest loss in his life, when his father Hermann died at age fifty-five. He had regarded his father as extremely friendly, mild, charming and a "good Man." Albert felt the loss for a long time, and went back to Italy to stay with his mother.

Several months later, he went back to Switzerland and married Mileva. In order to support his wife and himself, he applied for and was granted a job in the patent office in Switzerland. He was so involved with his atomic research, he had little time to bother with patents. As a result, no new patents were issued in the next four years. However, during these years, he published papers in electrodynamics, inertia, Browman movement, photo electronics and molecular dimensions. In spite of all this work, he still found time and energy to father a baby in 1904. As a result of all his study, he was convinced that the universe was not conceived and put together in a helter-skelter fashion by some accident. His further studies led to his understanding of time and space, which he called relativity. This means that our siblings, parents, uncles, aunts and cousins are floating around in space all the time, even if they appear to be on earth.

He also found that light from the sun takes eight minutes to reach the earth at the speed of 186,284 miles a second, which is faster than a sixteen year old boy with his cap on backwards can drive his souped up Studebaker.

In 1905, he developed the theory of "Equivalence of Mass and Energy." Energy has mass and mass has energy. If a body gives off energy E in the form of radiation, its mass (M) diminishes by EC2 (c=speed of light) proving that a tiny amount of mass can produce a tremendous amount of energy. M=E.C2.

One day while discussing energy to a class of students, he wrote the equation on the board and gave the above explanation. When he was finished, he asked if they all understood it. Only one student stood up and said he understood it and agrees with it. Einstein replied, "If you do, you're smarter than me." "I don't understand it." "I heard it last night on the Hi SCI FI channel. He was a real joker.

Although Einstein had been born to Jewish parents, he never became a practicing Jew, but when he perceived what was happening to the Jews in Germany after W.W.I, he had enough ethnic sympathy to embrace Zionism and assist Chaim Weizman in establishing Israel as a refuge from Germany anti-Semitism. In keeping with this effort, Einstein agreed to sail to the United States to try to interest Americans in Zionism and raise money to fund the enterprise. When he landed in New York, he was greeted with a massive outpouring that could only be matched by the Yankees bringing in the World Series. The visit was a huge success and established the foundation for later birth of the State of Israel.

In 1916, Einstein could not tolerate the hate and barbarity of the Germans, so he moved to Holland where he continued his scientific studies in a friendly, co-operative environment. The world war days were trying for him, but he completed some very important work during that period. Due to the extreme tension and worry that plagued him, he developed intractable stomach trouble. In spite of treatment with Propose and Medium, he did not respond well and his doctor prescribed total bed rest. Mileva was too involved with her own agenda, and was not able or willing to attend Albert's needs. Fortunately, he had an Uncle Randolph Einstein living close by with his daughter Elsa. They convinced Albert to move in with them, which he did after much persuasion. With good food, chicken soup and sympathetic care, he improved. After a few months, he felt well and comfortable so he agreed to stay on. He gave up on Mileva and asked for a divorce.

In the meantime, Elsa had been doing Albert's correspondence and typing his research notes on their computer. She, in turn, taught him to ad. When work on relativity was published and accepted by all the important scientific authorities, his success and fame were celebrated everywhere but Germany and Russia. The Germans, of course, resented the fact that a Jew was the first to conceive of relativity and not a "pure Aryan", and the Russians denounced it as bourgeois physics. In spite of these detractors, all the rest of the world appreciated him for what he was—a genius.

As he approached middle age, he was bothered by one problem. He had always been blessed with a full head of hair which was his trademark and for which he was very proud. However, as time went by, he became worried about a developing balding trait. When he noticed his hair was starting to fall out more rapidly, he became panicky. He tried some of the "snake Oil" remedies he saw on TV, but to no avail. Finally, he heard about a hair transplant specialist in Massachusetts, USA. He contacted this physician by E-Mail and arranged for a consultation. Einstein did not want his problem to be publicized, so he secretly traveled to the USA, and after a favorable examination, underwent a transplant procedure. He wanted to wait for healing to take place, so he took a room in Connecticut, near Foxwoods Casino and played the slot machines daily.

He had a successful run of the machines and won enough money to pay for his trip. The hair transplant "took" immediately, and the new hair started to grow on schedule and the new hair grew in, exactly replacing his lost hair, which was thick, bushy and white. No one ever knew the secret of Einstein's hair.

While he was in the U.S, he received offers from Universities all over the world to join their faculties, because Germany, now under Hitler's tyranny would not welcome him back into their country. While reviewing the offers, he decided to visit Princeton in New Jersey. He was delighted with the area as well as the liberal, progressive attitude of the school itself. He agreed to the offer, and was associated with the school's Institute for Advanced Study. He was always recognized when he walked in the town of Princeton, but the people were considerate enough not to bother him or ask stupid questions. However, when Elsa cared to join him, they found a perfect retreat in an estate in Old Lyme, Connecticut. They soon made friends and were living a "luxurious" life in America.

However, in Germany, Hitler had taken over power, and he vowed to rid Germany of all Jews whom he blamed for the sad plight of Germany. He took away businesses and possessions of Jews and confiscated their valuables. He closed schools and universities to them and would not allow Jewish doctors to treat Germans. This caused Einstein great sorrow, and he lent his name to organizations that would help the victims to escape to other lands. He felt guilty being unable to help personally, but he knew he would not be allowed to enter his old country.

He worked to promote the British protectors of Palestine to allow migration of German refugees, but the British Police would not allow them to enter. The resulting holocaust is well known and Albert Einstein was devastated. He spent his next years trying to promote peace. In 1944, a group of Jewish educators sponsored a secular university in Waltham, Mass. It was located near Harvard, Radcliff, MIT, Boston College, and many other fine educational institutions. It had the endorsement of Governor Tobin and Archbishop Cushing as well as Albert Einstein. His name lent credibility to the school that became recognized as a wonderful, well-staffed liberal college open to members of all sects and religions as long as the students were qualified. The school was named after Louis Brandies, Associate Justice of the Supreme Court from 1916-1939.

Albert Einstein lived out his life dedicated to supporting Israel and Brandeis while feeling guilty for promoting the building of the atomic bomb, which killed thousands of Japanese citizens. He had been involved with the development of the atomic bomb during World War II in the belief that Hitler was working on the production of nuclear weapons and had access to uranium in Czechoslovakia. On April 18, 1955 Albert Einstein died of a ruptured aortic aneurysm.

Printed in the United States
16103LVS00005B/574-576